For
Clare

First US edition 2021
First published by Berbay Publishing (Australia) 2019

Library of Congress Catalog Card Number 2021939353
ISBN 978-1-5362-1460-4

22 23 24 25 26 APS 10 9 8 7 6 5 4 3 2

Printed in Humen, Dongguan, China

This book was typeset in Passport.
The illustrations were done in watercolor and were
adapted from nineteenth-century artwork sourced from
*Animals: 1,419 Copyright-Free Illustrations of Mammals,
Birds, Fish, Insects, Etc.* (New York: Dover, 1979).

Candlewick Press
99 Dover Street
Somerville, Massachusetts 02144

www.candlewick.com

HEADS and TAILS UNDERWATER

John Canty

CANDLEWICK PRESS

I have ten legs.

I can nip you
with my claws.

I can walk
sideways.

I AM A . . .

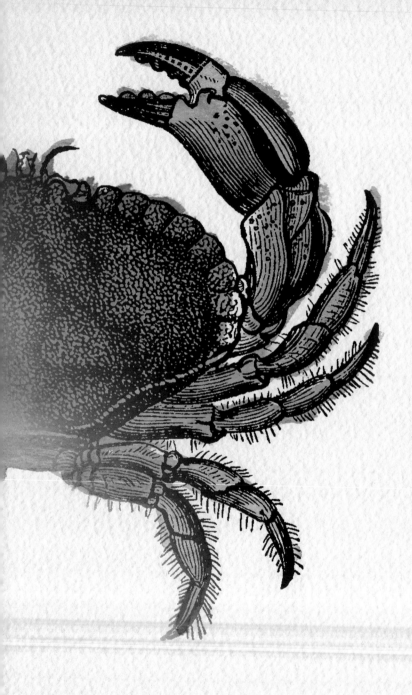

CRAB.

I look like a snake,
but I am a fish.

I am covered in
slippery slime.

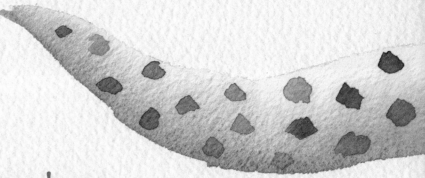

I live in salt water
or fresh water.

I AM AN...

EEL.

I have five arms.

I can regrow my
arms if I need to.

I live on the seabed
and on rocks.

I AM A . . .

STARFISH.

I am gentle.

I can sing.

I am the biggest
animal in the world.

I AM...

A . . .

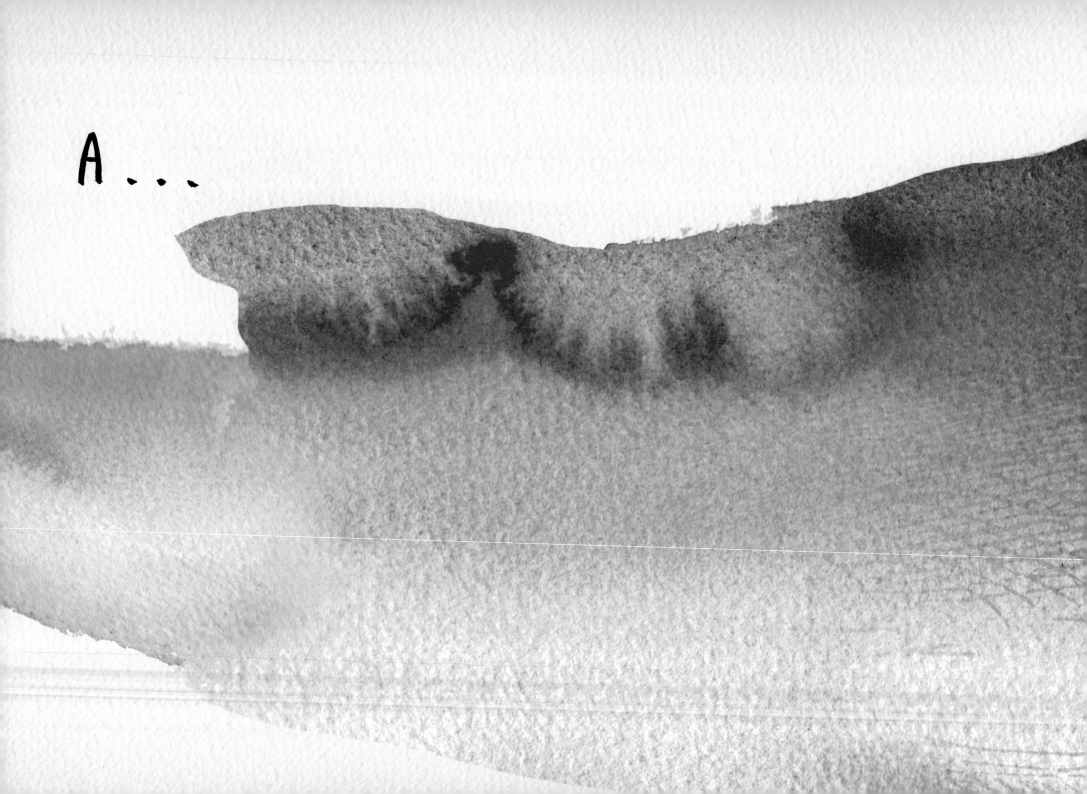

WHALE.

I have long tentacles
that can sting.

I don't have a brain.

I wobble
like jelly.

I AM A...

JELLYFISH.

I glide through
the ocean.

I have a wide
and flat body.

I have a dangerous
barbed tail.

I AM A...

STINGRAY.

I hatch from
an egg.

I lose my tail
as I grow.

I breathe underwater.

I AM A . . .

TADPOLE.

I can croak loudly.

I hop and jump from place to place.

I live on land and in water.

I AM...

FROG.

I can't swim
quickly.

I am a fish with
a horse-like face.

My daddy carried me
in his pouch when
I was a baby.

I AM A ...

SEAHORSE.

I have a hard shell
that covers my body.

I eat sea grass.

I travel long distances
to lay eggs on a beach.

I AM A ...

SEA TURTLE.

I have
three hearts.

I can change
color to hide.

I have eight long,
flexible arms.

I AM AN...

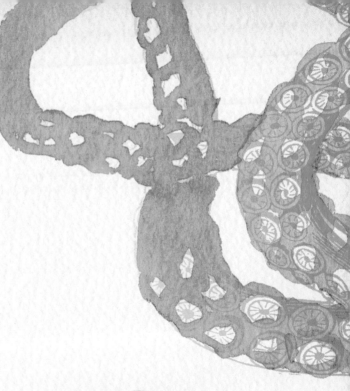
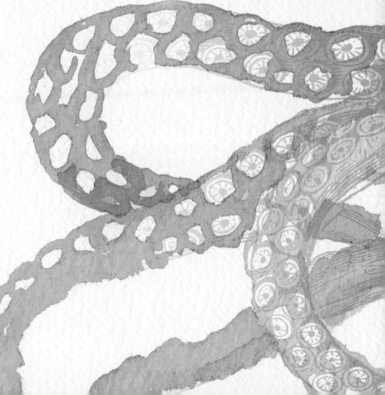

OCTOPUS.

I live around
coral reefs.

I swim in schools.

I have a long nose that
can reach into crevices.

I AM A . . .

BUTTERFLY
FISH.

SWIM!
SWIM!
HERE COMES A...

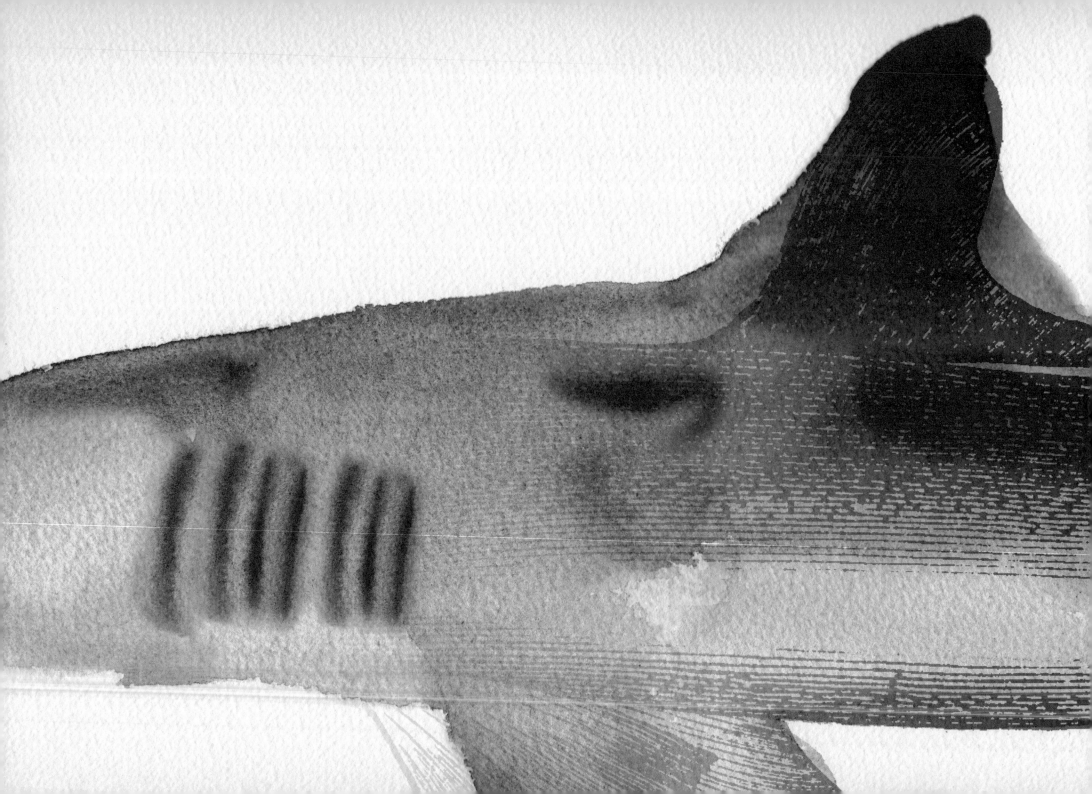

SHARK!